THE Los Angeles Dodgers

BY
MARK STEWART

New Hanover County Public Library
201 Chestnut Street
Wilmington, North Carolina 28401

NORWOOD HOUSE PRESS
CHICAGO, ILLINOIS

Norwood House Press
P.O. Box 316598
Chicago, Illinois 60631

For information regarding Norwood House Press, please visit our website at:
www.norwoodhousepress.com or call 866-565-2900.

All photos courtesy of Getty Images except the following:
Author's Collection (6, 33), Brooklyn Dodgers (7, 16), TCMA Ltd. (9),
Black Book Partners Archives (10, 11, 18, 25, 31, 36, 45), Tom DiPace (14), Bowman Gum Co. (15, 39),
Baseball Magazine (21), Macfadden Publications (22), SportsChrome (12, 23, 35 top right and bottom),
SSPC (24, 35 top left), The Sporting News (34 top), Old Judge & Gypsy Queen (34 bottom left),
Topps, Inc. (34 bottom right, 37 all, 41, 42 bottom, 43 both), Gum Inc. (38),
Audio Sports, Inc. (40), Louis Dormand (42 top), Matt Richman (48).
Cover Photo: Hannah Foslien/Getty Images

The memorabilia and artifacts pictured in this book are presented for educational and informational purposes,
and come from the collection of the author.

Editor: Mike Kennedy
Designer: Ron Jaffe
Project Management: Black Book Partners, LLC.
Special thanks to Topps, Inc.

Library of Congress Cataloging-in-Publication Data

Stewart, Mark, 1960-
    The Los Angeles Dodgers / by Mark Stewart.
       p. cm. -- (Team spirit)
    Includes bibliographical references and index.
    Summary: "A Team Spirit Baseball edition featuring the Los Angeles Dodgers
that chronicles the history and accomplishments of the team. Includes access
to the Team Spirit website, which provides additional information, updates
and photos"--Provided by publisher.
    ISBN 978-1-59953-486-2 (library : alk. paper) -- ISBN 978-1-60357-366-5
(ebook) 1. Los Angeles Dodgers (Baseball team)--History--Juvenile
literature. I. Title.
    GV875.L6S82 2012
    796.357'640979494--dc23
                                                          2011047962

Manufactured in the United States of America in North Mankato, Minnesota.
196N—012012

COVER PHOTO: The Dodgers jump for joy after a win in 2011.

TABLE OF CONTENTS

ABOUT OUR GLOSSARY

In this book, there may be several words that you are reading for the first time. Some are sports words, some are new vocabulary words, and some are familiar words that are used in an unusual way. All of these words are defined on page 46. Throughout the book, sports words appear in **bold type**. Regular vocabulary words appear in ***bold italic type***.

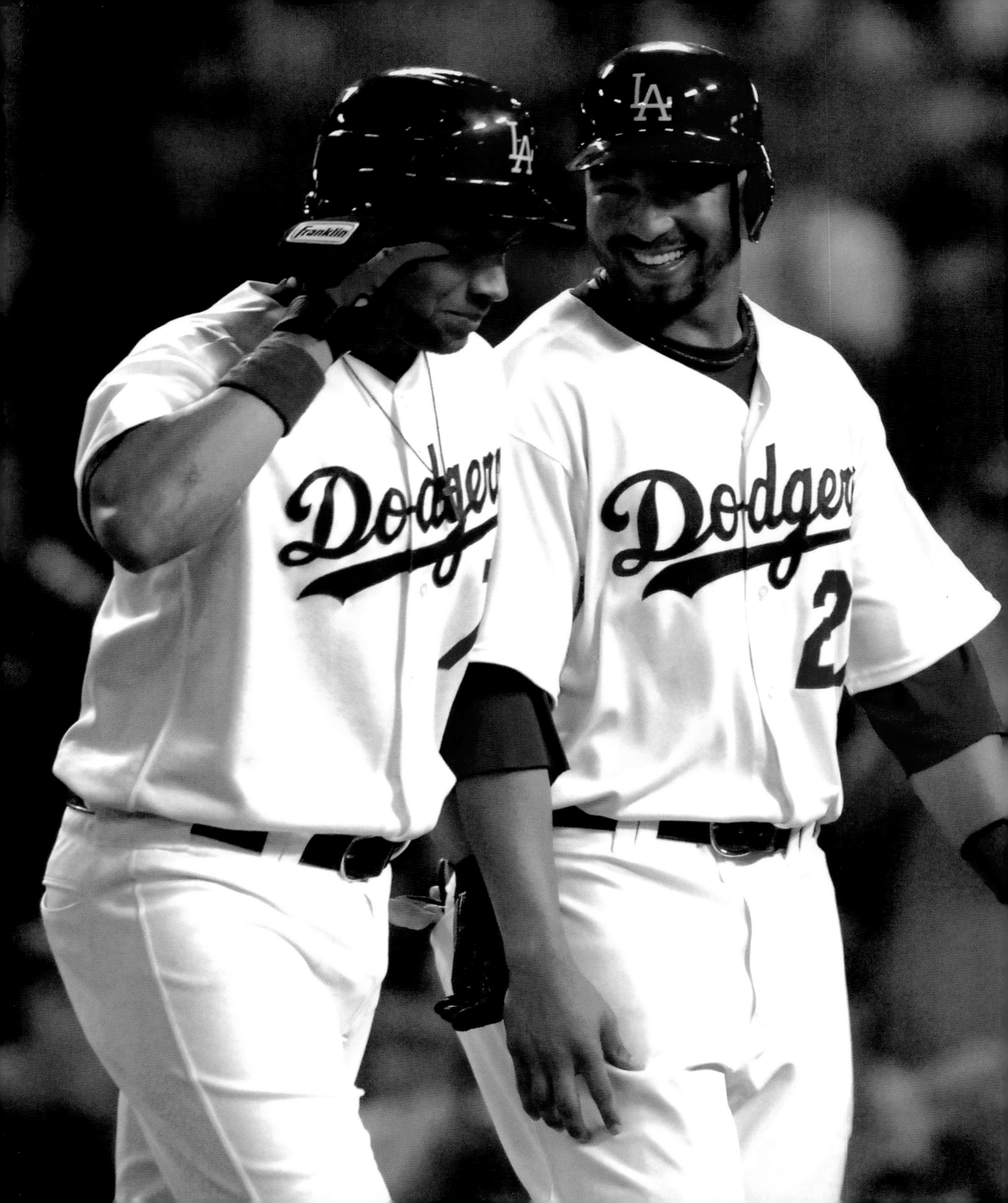
LA
Franklin
Dodgers
LA
Dodgers

MEET THE DODGERS

Wherever you go in the world, chances are that you won't have to look too hard to find a fan of the Los Angeles Dodgers. There are millions in California, and millions more around the globe. All have one thing in common—they proudly "bleed" Dodger blue.

People love the Dodgers for different reasons. The team is known for giving young players a chance to become stars, and for giving older players a second chance. The Dodgers were the last baseball team to play in Brooklyn, New York and the first to play in Southern California.

This book tells the story of the Dodgers. They have won championships on the East Coast and the West Coast. They have had amazing victories and heartbreaking defeats. And most important, their players have changed the face of baseball.

James Loney and Matt Kemp return to the dugout after a home run.
The Dodgers gave these young players a chance and both became stars.

GLORY DAYS

For more than half of their history, the Dodgers were based in Brooklyn, New York. People were accustomed to watching good baseball there long before the team played its first game. In fact, the best clubs and players had been meeting in Brooklyn starting in the 1850s. When the Dodgers first took the field in 1884, fans expected this *tradition* to continue.

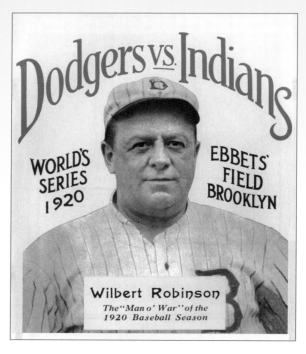

Dodgers vs. Indians
WORLD'S SERIES 1920
EBBETS FIELD BROOKLYN
Wilbert Robinson
The "Man o' War" of the 1920 Baseball Season

The team went through several names in its first few seasons, including the Atlantics and Grays. They eventually were nicknamed the Dodgers in honor of Brooklyn's *pedestrians*, who had to dodge the trolleys that crisscrossed the city's avenues and streets. In 1888, the team was renamed the Bridegrooms, after several of its players had weddings. The Bridegrooms were members of the **American Association (AA)**. In 1890, they decided to join the rival **National League (NL)**. They won the **pennant** in their first year in the league.

Brooklyn's stars included Willie Keeler, Joe Kelley, Hughie Jennings, Bill Dahlen, Fielder Jones, Brickyard Kennedy, and Joe McGinnity. The team's owner was Charles Ebbets, who started his career as a peanut vendor and ticket-taker. In 1913, Ebbets built a "baseball palace" for the Dodgers and named it Ebbets Field. By this time, fans were calling the team the Robins in honor of Wilbert Robinson, Brooklyn's popular manager. "Uncle Robbie" led the club to the pennant in 1916 and 1920.

Brooklyn struggled during the 1920s and 1930s, before rising to the top of the NL in 1941. Known as the Dodgers once again, the team starred Pete Reiser, Dolph Camilli, Kirby Higbe, and Whit Wyatt. From 1947 to 1956, the Dodgers were the best team

LEFT: Wilbert Robinson managed the Dodgers to two pennants.
ABOVE: Dolph Camilli led the NL in home runs in 1941.

in the NL. They won six pennants during that time.

Something more important set the Dodgers apart, however. In the 1940s, they changed the face of baseball by signing the first African-American stars. The man who broke baseball's "color barrier" was Jackie Robinson. He would eventually be elected to the **Hall of Fame**.

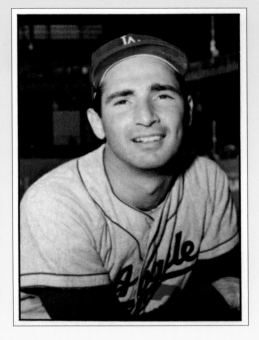

In addition to Robinson, the Dodgers were led by Duke Snider, Roy Campanella, Pee Wee Reese, Gil Hodges, Don Newcombe, and Carl Erskine. Campanella and Newcombe were African-Americans. Brooklyn won its only **World Series** in 1955, against the New York Yankees.

In 1958, the people of Brooklyn were shocked when team owner Walter O'Malley announced that the Dodgers were moving to Los Angeles, California. Baseball fans on the West Coast were *ecstatic*. They had wanted their own **big-league** club for 20 years. With pitchers Don Drysdale and Sandy Koufax leading the way, the Dodgers won the World Series in 1959, 1963, and 1965.

LEFT: Jackie Robinson broke baseball's color barrier in 1947, and then made the Dodgers the top team in the league.   **ABOVE**: Sandy Koufax pitched the Dodgers to three championships.

9

A new *generation* of Dodgers starred for the team in the 1970s. For many years, the Los Angeles infield featured Steve Garvey, Davey Lopes, Bill Russell, and Ron Cey—four of the league's best players. In the 1980s, Dodgers fans cheered for Fernando Valenzuela, Pedro Guerrero, Orel Hershiser, Mike Scioscia, Steve Sax, and Kirk Gibson. The Dodgers continued their winning ways, becoming World Series champions in 1981 and 1988.

After winning at least two pennants in each *decade* from the 1940s to the 1980s, the Dodgers failed to reach the World Series during the 1990s. Still, they were in the running almost every year, thanks to sluggers Mike Piazza and Eric Karros, speedy Brett Butler, and hard-throwing Ramon Martinez.

As Los Angeles continued to find new talent, the team hoped to be the first to win championships in three different centuries.

Among the Dodgers' top hitters were Adrian Beltre, Shawn Green, Russell Martin, Rafael Furcal, Andre Ethier, and Matt Kemp. Their best pitchers included Eric Gagne, Jonathan Broxton, Hiroki Kuroda, and Clayton Kershaw. The Dodgers made it to the **playoffs** four times from 2004 to 2009. However, each time they fell short of their goal to win a championship.

Of course, the great thing about being a Dodgers fan is the old saying, "Wait 'til next year!" The team does its best to put winning players on the field every season. The players do their best to uphold the team's winning tradition. When you root for a baseball team, you can't ask for more than that.

LEFT: Orel Hershiser delivers a pitch.
ABOVE: Jonathan Broxton was one of baseball's hardest throwers.

HOME TURF

In the 1800s, the Dodgers played in Washington Park in Brooklyn. It was built on the site of George Washington's headquarters during the **Battle of Long Island**. The actual building he used served as the ladies' restroom. From 1913 to 1957, the Dodgers made Ebbets Field their home. The stadium is remembered for its beautiful marble main entrance and for the sign in right field that advertised a clothing store. Any batter who hit the sign with a batted ball won a free suit.

The Dodgers' current home sits on a hill with views of downtown Los Angeles and the San Gabriel Mountains. It was built in 1962 and was the first ballpark to draw three million fans in one season. The stadium is famous for its grilled Dodger Dogs, which some say are the best in baseball.

BY THE NUMBERS

- The Dodgers' stadium has 56,000 seats.
- The distance from home plate to the left field foul pole is 330 feet.
- The distance from home plate to the center field fence is 395 feet.
- The distance from home plate to the right field fence is 330 feet.

The fans stand and sing the national anthem at Dodger Stadium.

DRESSED FOR SUCCESS

The Dodgers' colors since the early 1900s have been blue and white. Over the years, other colors were added and subtracted, and the shade of blue changed from navy blue to a lighter royal blue. In 1916, the team tried a very unusual checked pattern of thin blue lines—and won the pennant!

FURILLO

Until the early 1930s, the Dodgers usually wore a large *B* on their uniforms and caps. At the end of the 1930s, the team switched to script lettering that spelled out *Dodgers* on its home uniforms and *Brooklyn* on its road uniforms. A red uniform number was added on the front during the 1950s. Except for the interlocking *LA* on their caps, the Dodgers have kept the same basic look for more than 50 years.

LEFT: Andre Ethier takes a swing in the team's 2011 road uniform.
ABOVE: Carl Furillo's 1955 Brooklyn uniform features the same team colors.

WE WON!

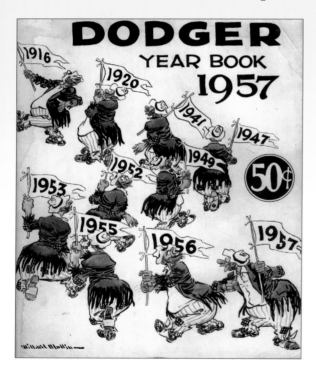

The Dodgers had many great teams when they played in Brooklyn. But the first seven times they went to the World Series, they did not win the championship. Dodgers fans were also disappointed when they lost the pennant in a pair of tie-breaking playoff series in 1946 and 1951. The people of Brooklyn never gave up hope. They were famous for saying, "Wait 'til next year."

In 1955, next year finally arrived. Duke Snider, Roy Campanella, Jackie Robinson, Pee Wee Reese, Gil Hodges, Carl Furillo, and Don Newcombe powered the Dodgers to the pennant. However, in the World Series against the New York Yankees, it was 21-year-old pitcher Johnny Podres and part-time outfielder Sandy Amoros who took center stage and led the team to its one and only Brooklyn championship.

In 1959, another surprise star helped the Dodgers win the World Series. Larry Sherry won two games against the Chicago White Sox and **saved** two others. The unexpected batting leader was second baseman Charlie Neal, who had ten hits and six **runs batted in (RBIs)**.

The team's 1963 championship was surprising too, but for a different reason. The Dodgers faced the Yankees in a series that most fans expected to be very close. Instead, the Dodgers swept New York in four games. Sandy Koufax was the star. After winning 25 games during the season, he won twice more against the Yankees. Koufax also starred in the 1965 World Series against the Minnesota Twins. He pitched **shutouts** in Game 5 and Game 7 to give Los Angeles its third championship in seven seasons.

The Dodgers played in four more World Series from 1966 to 1978, but they lost each time. Their next championship did not come until 1981. Again, the Dodgers faced the Yankees. After losing the first two games, Los Angeles won the next four. Ron Cey, Steve Yeager, and Pedro Guerrero led the hitting attack, and Fernando Valenzuela, Jerry Reuss, and Steve Howe were the star pitchers.

Of all the team's World Series championships, the victory in 1988 over the Oakland A's was the most magical. Kirk Gibson, the NL **Most Valuable Player (MVP)** that season, had injured himself in the playoffs. He told manager Tommy Lasorda that he could give him just a few good swings, and that was it. Gibson used his lone trip to the plate to blast the winning home run in Game 1. Many baseball fans believe this was the greatest home run of the last 30 years.

Orel Hershiser took the mound for Game 2. He allowed just three hits in a 6–0 victory. Oakland won the next game, but Los Angeles took the final two. Hershiser got the win in Game 5 and was voted the MVP of the World Series.

As for Gibson, he was true to his word. His pinch-hit homer was his one and only appearance. However, Mickey Hatcher batted .368 in Gibson's place. Hatcher hit two home runs against the luckless A's—one more than he had hit during the entire regular season!

GO-TO GUYS

To be a true star in baseball, you need more than a quick bat and a strong arm. You have to be a "go-to guy"—someone the manager wants on the pitcher's mound or in the batter's box when it matters most. Fans of the Dodgers have had a lot to cheer about over the years, including these great stars …

 ## THE PIONEERS

JAKE DAUBERT   First Baseman

• BORN: 4/7/1884   • DIED: 10/9/1924   • PLAYED FOR TEAM: 1910 TO 1918

Jake Daubert was the finest all-around first baseman of his time. He was a smooth fielder and smart hitter. Daubert could crash long drives, but he was also a magician when it came to bunting. He was the NL's batting champion in 1913 and 1914.

PEE WEE REESE   Shortstop

• BORN: 7/23/1918   • DIED: 8/14/1999
• PLAYED FOR TEAM: 1940 TO 1942 & 1946 TO 1958

Pee Wee Reese was the captain of the Dodgers in the 1940s and 1950s. He was one of the game's best shortstops and an excellent **leadoff hitter**.

DAZZY VANCE   Pitcher

- BORN: 3/4/1891   • DIED: 2/16/1961
- PLAYED FOR TEAM: 1922 TO 1932 & 1935

Dazzy Vance was the league's hardest-throwing pitcher. He led the NL in strikeouts seven years in a row and was its top winner in 1924 and 1925.

JACKIE ROBINSON   Second Baseman

- BORN: 1/31/1919   • DIED: 10/24/1972
- PLAYED FOR TEAM: 1947 TO 1956

Jackie Robinson was a fierce competitor. In 1947, he became the first African-American player in the big leagues in the 20th century. Robinson led the Dodgers to the pennant in his first season and was the NL MVP in his third.

DUKE SNIDER   Outfielder

- BORN: 9/19/1926   • DIED: 2/27/2011   • PLAYED FOR TEAM: 1947 TO 1962

Duke Snider was one of the NL's most feared left-handed sluggers. He was a fast and graceful outfielder, with a strong and accurate arm. Snider hit 326 homers during the 1950s—more than anyone else in baseball.

ROY CAMPANELLA   Catcher

- BORN: 11/19/1921   • DIED: 6/26/1993   • PLAYED FOR TEAM: 1948 TO 1957

Roy Campanella was a great hitter and fielder who won three NL MVP awards during the 1950s. His career was cut short by a car accident after the 1957 season, and he spent the rest of his life in a wheelchair.

ABOVE: Dazzy Vance

SANDY KOUFAX   Pitcher

- BORN: 12/30/1935 • PLAYED FOR TEAM: 1955 TO 1966

Sandy Koufax struggled with his control early in his career. Once he started throwing more strikes, he became a superstar. Koufax pitched a **no-hitter** each year from 1962 to 1965 and led the NL in victories three times.

DON DRYSDALE   Pitcher

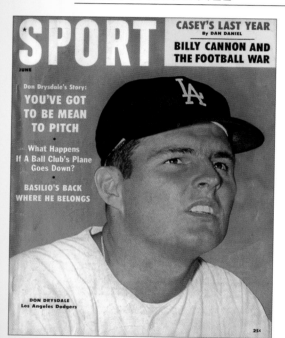

SPORT

JUNE

CASEY'S LAST YEAR
By DAN DANIEL

BILLY CANNON AND THE FOOTBALL WAR

Don Drysdale's Story:
YOU'VE GOT TO BE MEAN TO PITCH

- What Happens If A Ball Club's Plane Goes Down?

BASILIO'S BACK WHERE HE BELONGS

DON DRYSDALE
Los Angeles Dodgers

25¢

- BORN: 7/23/1936 • DIED: 7/3/1993
- PLAYED FOR TEAM: 1956 TO 1969

Don Drysdale threw a sidearm fastball that moved suddenly as it neared the batter. He was known for pitching inside to hitters, so it was not a good idea to stand too close to home plate. In 1968, Drysdale pitched six shutouts in a row.

OREL HERSHISER   Pitcher

- BORN: 9/16/1958
- PLAYED FOR TEAM: 1983 TO 1994 & 2000

It would be hard for a player to have a better year than Orel Hershiser did in 1988. He won 23 games and finished the season with 59 scoreless innings to set a record. In the World Series, Hershiser won two games, gave up only two runs, and batted 1.000!

MIKE PIAZZA   Catcher

- BORN: 9/4/1968   • PLAYED FOR TEAM: 1992 TO 1998

Mike Piazza was **drafted** by the Dodgers in the 62nd round as a favor to a family friend. Piazza returned the favor by becoming the greatest hitting catcher in history. His .362 batting average in 1997 was the highest in the last 100 years for a National Leaguer at his position.

MATT KEMP   Outfielder

- BORN: 9/23/1984
- FIRST YEAR WITH TEAM: 2006

The most dangerous hitters combine great speed and power. That's what made Matt Kemp so scary. In 2011, he stole 40 bases and led the NL with 39 home runs and 126 RBIs.

CLAYTON KERSHAW   Pitcher

- BORN: 3/19/1988
- FIRST YEAR WITH TEAM: 2008

Clayton Kershaw was the youngest player in baseball when the Dodgers first handed him the ball in 2008. In 2011, he led the NL with 21 wins and struck out 248 batters—the most by a Dodger since Sandy Koufax. Kershaw finished the year by winning the **Cy Young Award**.

LEFT: Don Drysdale
RIGHT: Matt Kemp

The Dodgers have had some of baseball's finest managers during their long history, including Ned Hanlon, Wilbert Robinson, Leo Durocher, Burt Shotton, Charlie Dressen, Davey Johnson, Joe Torre, and Don Mattingly. The team's two best managers were Walt Alston and Tommy Lasorda.

Alston was in charge of the club from 1954 to 1976. He was a quiet leader who never panicked. He always found a way to get the most out of his teams. In the days before video and computerized statistics,

Alston was very good at studying opponents and then remembering the tiniest details about them. He used this information to win close games. Alston was also a good teacher. In fact, he was a schoolteacher between seasons before becoming the Dodgers' manager.

Lasorda coached third base for Alston for four seasons. During that time, many teams wanted to hire Lasorda as their manager. He stayed loyal to the Dodgers, and near the end of the 1976 season

LEFT: Walt Alston managed the Dodgers in Brooklyn and Los Angeles.
RIGHT: Tommy Lasorda won four pennants as the team's manager.

he took over after Alston retired. Lasorda led the Dodgers to the NL pennant in 1977 and 1978, and again in 1981. That year they beat the New York Yankees to win the World Series.

Lasorda was Alston's opposite. He was very emotional. His players loved him because he was their biggest cheerleader. Lasorda led the Dodgers to three more NL West titles in the 1980s. In 1988, they returned to the World Series. Lasorda made all the right moves. No one thought Los Angeles could beat the Oakland A's, but Lasorda and his players made it look easy!

When it came to calling the shots in the team's business office, few people had a greater impact on the Dodgers—or on baseball—than Branch Rickey. Rickey ran the team during the 1940s. As a young man, he had watched helplessly as an African-American friend and teammate was forced off his college baseball team. Rickey vowed that he would *integrate* baseball someday. In 1947, he promoted Jackie Robinson to the big leagues and broke the game's unwritten rule banning non-white players.

ONE GREAT DAY

When Jackie Robinson stepped on the field for his first official game as a member of the Dodgers, it was a great day for baseball. It was also a great day for America. For the first time in the 20th century, an African-American was in uniform for a big-league game. Although there was never an official rule against signing African-American players, team owners had kept them out of baseball for generations.

This was not only an injustice, it robbed the game of some wonderful players. The same was true in American society, where African-Americans were rarely allowed to compete or contribute on the same level as whites. Attitudes finally began to change during **World War II**, when people of all colors died for freedom. How could members of any race be denied equality after fighting for their country?

Branch Rickey, the boss of the Dodgers, signed Robinson to a contract. Rickey warned his new star that he would face prejudice

Spider Jorgensen, Pee Wee Reese, Eddie Stanky, and Jackie Robinson
made up Brooklyn's starting infield on April 15, 1947.

from fans and opposing players—and even teammates. Robinson agreed to play hard and resist the temptation to fight back.

Robinson played first base and batted second for the Dodgers on Opening Day against the Boston Braves. Brooklyn won 5–3. Although Robinson did not get a hit, it was still an unforgettable day for him and baseball.

Robinson led the NL in stolen bases in 1947 and helped the Dodgers win the pennant. They would win five more in his 10-year career. During that time, some of baseball's greatest stars walked through the door that Robinson opened, including Hank Aaron, Ernie Banks, Frank Robinson, Roy Campanella, and Willie Mays.

LEGEND HAS IT

WHO WAS THE FIRST AFRICAN-AMERICAN MANAGER IN 'WHITE' BASEBALL?

LEGEND HAS IT that Roy Campanella was. In 1946, he was playing for the Dodgers' **minor-league** team in Nashua, New Hampshire. When manager Walt Alston was ejected prior to a game against the Lawrence Millionaires, he handed the lineup card to Campanella and told him to manage the team. Campanella led his club to a 7–5 victory.

ABOVE: Jackie Robinson chats with Roy Campanella. Both were baseball ground-breakers.

WHO WAS THE DODGERS 'MOST PERFECT' PITCHER?

LEGEND HAS IT that Clayton Kershaw was. Sandy Koufax made headlines when he threw a **perfect game** against the Chicago Cubs in 1965. But Kershaw did even better as a high-school pitcher in 2006. Against Northwest High in a big playoff contest, he faced 21 batters in the seven-inning game and struck out every one. Not a single Northwest player hit a fair ball against him. You can't get much more perfect than that!

DID A PRACTICAL JOKE ONCE HELP THE DODGERS BECOME CHAMPIONS?

LEGEND HAS IT that it did. A practical joke is a funny trick played on someone by friends or teammates. During spring training in 1988, the Dodgers "welcomed" their newest player, Kirk Gibson, by putting shoe polish on the inside of his batting helmet. When Gibson took it off, there was a black ring around his head. Gibson surprised his giggling teammates when he became furious. He had come to the team to win, not to fool around! From that moment on, the players got serious and followed Gibson's lead—all the way to the championship.

The 1981 baseball season was like no other. It had a player strike. The team with the most wins did not make it into the playoffs. The teams that did qualify for the **postseason** had to play two rounds for the first time in history. But when all was said and done, what fans remember most about the 1981 season was a round-faced, 20-year-old Mexican pitcher named Fernando Valenzuela.

Valenzuela started the year with a shutout of the Houston Astros. Next he beat the San Francisco Giants. In his next three starts, he blanked the San Diego Padres, and then did the same to the Astros and Giants again. Suddenly baseball fans "discovered" Valenzuela. Wherever he pitched, people streamed into the ballpark in huge numbers. Fernando-Mania had begun!

The more people saw of the left-hander, the more they liked him. Before throwing a pitch, he spun around so his back faced the batter. And he seemed to look toward the sky instead of home plate. No one had ever seen a pitcher like him before. Valenzuela won eight times in a row before the Dodgers finally lost a game he pitched. By then,

Fernando Valenzuela awaits a pitch in batting practice. It seemed there was nothing he couldn't do in 1981.

he was a worldwide celebrity. The only thing that could stop Valenzuela was an argument between owners and players that cancelled games for two months beginning in June. When the season restarted, Valenzuela pitched three more shutouts. All told, he led the major leagues in innings pitched, strikeouts, **complete games**, and shutouts.

At the end of the season, Valenzuela helped the Dodgers win their first championship since the 1960s. He was the youngest pitcher ever to start Game 1 of a World Series. Later, he was named the **Rookie of the Year** and winner of the Cy Young Award. No one had ever claimed both in the same season. To top it all off, Valenzuela also won the Silver Slugger award as the NL's best-hitting pitcher!

TEAM SPIRIT

During their days in Brooklyn, the Dodgers and their fans rewrote the book on team spirit. Many players lived right in the neighborhood where Ebbets Field was located and walked to the ballpark. Their friends and neighbors filled the stands. The most famous fan was Hilda Chester. She sat in the outfield and had a voice like a foghorn. Everyone knew when Hilda was happy or mad about the team.

The fans in Los Angeles are a little different. Because the city is the center of the movie business, there are always famous actors and actresses in the stands. Some fans spend almost as much time trying to spot celebrities as they do watching the action. They don't have to look very hard. On many nights, show business stars are asked to throw out the first pitch.

LEFT: Tickets to a Dodgers game let fans do a little celebrity-watching.
ABOVE: This souvenir pin was sold at Ebbets Field in the 1950s.

TIMELINE

This guidebook shows the Dodger "bum" in his new Southern California wardrobe.

BASEBALL OFFICIAL GUIDE
USEN'T YOUSE T' LIVE IN BROOKYN?
1960 Edition RULES and AVERAGES Compiled by J. G. TAYLOR SPINK $1.00
PUBLISHED BY The Sporting News

1920
Wilbert Robinson leads the team to the World Series.

1930
Babe Herman sets a team record with a .393 batting average.

1958
The Dodgers play their first season in Los Angeles.

1890
The team wins the pennant in its first NL season.

1947
Jackie Robinson breaks baseball's color barrier.

1955
The Dodgers win their first World Series.

CARUTHERS, (P. Brooklyn)

Bob Caruthers won 23 games for the 1890 team.

OLD JUDGE & GYPSY QUEEN CIGARETTES

Gil Hodges was the hitting hero in Game 7 of the 1955 World Series.

GIL Hodges
BROOKLYN DODGERS 1st BASE

Steve Yeager hit two homers in the 1981 World Series.

Eric Gagne

1981
The Dodgers win the World Series for the fourth time.

1996
A Dodger is named Rookie of the Year for the fifth time in a row.

2003
Eric Gagne saves 55 games and wins the Cy Young Award.

1963
The Dodgers sweep the New York Yankees in the World Series.

1988
Orel Hershiser and Kirk Gibson lead the Dodgers to victory in the World Series.

2011
Clayton Kershaw wins the Cy Young Award.

Clayton Kershaw

FUN FACTS

HOMER CRAZY

In a 2006 game with the San Diego Padres, the Dodgers set a record with four home runs in a row in the ninth inning. The Dodgers tied the score at 7–7 and won in the 10th inning with another home run.

IT TAKES A THIEF

In 1962, Maury Wills became the first player in history to steal 100 bases in a season, with 104. No one in the NL had stolen more than 50 bases since 1923.

YOUTH IS SERVED

During the player shortages caused by World War II, the Dodgers had 12 teenagers in uniform. The youngest was a shortstop named Tommy Brown, who was only 16 when he played for Brooklyn in 1944.

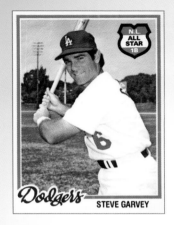

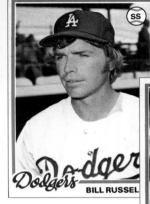

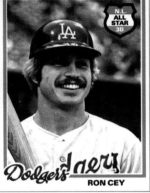

STEVE GARVEY

DAVE LOPES

BILL RUSSELL

RON CEY

FOUR-EVER TOGETHER

Steve Garvey, Davey Lopes, Bill Russell, and Ron Cey started for the Dodgers from 1973 to 1981. No other group of infielders has ever played together that long.

LONG DAY FOR LEON

In 1920, Brooklyn played a 26-inning game in Boston against the Braves. The game ended in a 1–1 tie and is still the longest game in big-league history. Leon Cadore pitched all 26 innings for Brooklyn.

ZACK ATTACK

The team's greatest star during its early years was Zack Wheat. The graceful outfielder played 18 seasons for Brooklyn and was the 1918 NL batting champion. Wheat still holds the team's career records for games, hits, doubles, and triples.

LEFT: Russell Martin hit the third of four homers against the San Diego Padres in 2006.   **ABOVE**: Steve Garvey, Davey Lopes, Bill Russell, and Ron Cey made up the Dodgers infield for nine years.

"We were all Americans, all teammates, all equal."
▶ **JACKIE ROBINSON**, ON THE 1947 DODGERS

"There are never-ending challenges. You never have the game perfected."
▶ **MIKE PIAZZA**, ON WHY HE WORKED SO HARD

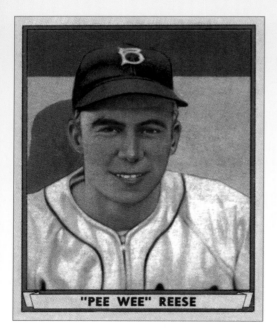

"PEE WEE" REESE

"I bleed Dodger blue and when I die, I'm going to the big Dodger in the sky."
▶ **TOMMY LASORDA**, ON HIS DEVOTION TO THE DODGERS

"Brooklyn was the most wonderful city a man could play in, and the fans there were the most loyal there were."
▶ **PEE WEE REESE**, ON PLAYING FOR THE DODGERS BEFORE THEY MOVED TO LOS ANGELES

"The best players in baseball get to the World Series, and that's what I'm trying to do."

▶ **MATT KEMP**, ON WHAT DRIVES HIM TO SUCCEED

"I really love baseball—the guys and the game. And I love the challenge of describing things."

▶ **VIN SCULLY**, ON ANNOUNCING DODGERS GAMES

"Baseball is a game of inches."

▶ **BRANCH RICKEY**, ON THE THIN LINE BETWEEN WINNING AND LOSING

"When they tore down Ebbets Field, they tore down a little piece of me."

▶ **DUKE SNIDER**, ON HIS FAVORITE STADIUM

"The greatest reward was winning. With the Dodgers, we did that a lot."

▶ **DON NEWCOMBE**, ON HIS FAVORITE PART OF PLAYING FOR BROOKLYN

LEFT: Pee Wee Reese
RIGHT: Don Newcombe

GREAT DEBATES

People who root for the Dodgers love to compare their favorite moments, teams, and players. Some debates have been going on for years! How would you settle these classic baseball arguments?

RUNNING

Record/Booklet on Baseball Fundamentals

MAURY WILLS WAS THE BEST BASERUNNER IN TEAM HISTORY ...

… because he led the league in stolen bases six years in a row. Wills (**LEFT**) stole 94 bases in 1965 and 104 in 1962. (He also won the NL MVP award in 1962!) The job of a leadoff hitter is to get into scoring position, and no Dodger did that better than Wills.

NO ONE WAS SCARIER ON THE BASEPATHS THAN JACKIE ROBINSON ...

… because he was fast and unpredictable. Robinson would steal any base at any time, including home. In fact, his steal of home in Game 1 of the 1955 World Series sent a message to the New York Yankees—*we're not scared of you!* The Dodgers lost that game but went on to win the championship. And by the way, Robinson scored more than 100 runs six times.

KIRK GIBSON'S HOMER IN THE 1988 WORLD SERIES WAS THE GREATEST IN TEAM HISTORY ...

... because it won the opening game and gave the Dodgers confidence to beat the mighty Oakland A's in the World Series. Gibson was too hurt to do more than pinch-hit. The Dodgers saved him to bat against Dennis Eckersley with the game on the line. Even after the ball flew into the stands, Gibson could barely run around the bases. Dodgers fans still get tears in their eyes when they remember Gibson's homer.

THEY WOULD HAVE NOTHING TO CRY ABOUT IF IT WEREN'T FOR MIKE SCIOSCIA'S HOME RUN SIX DAYS EARLIER ...

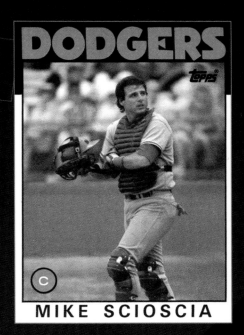

MIKE SCIOSCIA

... because that was the hit that got the Dodgers into the World Series that fall. Scioscia (RIGHT) came to bat in Game 4 of the **National League Championship Series (NLCS)** with the New York Mets leading 4–2 in the ninth inning. Dwight Gooden hadn't allowed a hit since the first inning. Scioscia had hit only three home runs all season. No one expected a long ball from him. But that's what happened. Scioscia tied the score with a two-run blast into the right field seats. The Dodgers went on to win the game and the series.

FOR THE RECORD

The great Dodgers teams and players have left their marks on the record books. These are the "best of the best" ...

Mike Marshall

Mike Piazza

DODGERS AWARD WINNERS

WINNER	AWARD	YEAR
Dolph Camilli	Most Valuable Player	1941
Jackie Robinson	Rookie of the Year	1947
Don Newcombe	Rookie of the Year	1949
Jackie Robinson	Most Valuable Player	1949
Roy Campanella	Most Valuable Player	1951
Joe Black	Rookie of the Year	1952
Jim Gilliam	Rookie of the Year	1953
Roy Campanella	Most Valuable Player	1953
Roy Campanella	Most Valuable Player	1955
Don Newcombe	Cy Young Award	1956
Don Newcombe	Most Valuable Player	1956
Frank Howard	Rookie of the Year	1960
Don Drysdale	Cy Young Award	1962
Maury Wills	Most Valuable Player	1962
Sandy Koufax	Cy Young Award	1963
Sandy Koufax	Most Valuable Player	1963
Jim Lefebvre	Rookie of the Year	1965
Sandy Koufax	Cy Young Award	1965
Sandy Koufax	Cy Young Award	1966
Ted Sizemore	Rookie of the Year	1969
Mike Marshall	Cy Young Award	1974
Steve Garvey	Most Valuable Player	1974
Rick Sutcliffe	Rookie of the Year	1979
Steve Howe	Rookie of the Year	1980
Fernando Valenzuela	Rookie of the Year	1981
Fernando Valenzuela	Cy Young Award	1981
Steve Sax	Rookie of the Year	1982
Orel Hershiser	Cy Young Award	1988
Kirk Gibson	Most Valuable Player	1988
Eric Karros	Rookie of the Year	1992
Mike Piazza	Rookie of the Year	1993
Raul Mondesi	Rookie of the Year	1994
Hideo Nomo	Rookie of the Year	1995
Todd Hollandsworth	Rookie of the Year	1996
Eric Gagne	Cy Young Award	2003
Clayton Kershaw	Cy Young Award	2011

DODGERS ACHIEVEMENTS

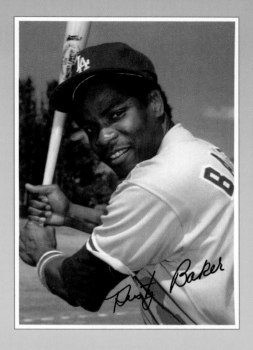

ACHIEVEMENT	YEAR
AA Pennant Winner	1889
NL Pennant Winner	1890
NL Pennant Winner	1899
NL Pennant Winner	1900
NL Pennant Winner	1916
NL Pennant Winner	1920
NL Pennant Winner	1941
NL Pennant Winner	1947
NL Pennant Winner	1949
NL Pennant Winner	1952
NL Pennant Winner	1953
NL Pennant Winner	1955
World Series Champions	1955
NL Pennant Winner	1959
World Series Champions	1959
NL Pennant Winner	1963
World Series Champions	1963
NL Pennant Winner	1965
World Series Champions	1965
NL Pennant Winner	1966
NL West Champions	1974
NL Pennant Winner	1974
NL West Champions	1977
NL Pennant Winner	1977
NL West Champions	1978
NL Pennant Winner	1978
NL West Champions	1981
NL Pennant Winner	1981
World Series Champions	1981
NL West Champions	1983
NL West Champions	1985
NL West Champions	1988
NL Pennant Winner	1988
World Series Champions	1988
NL West Champions	1995
NL West Champions	2004
NL West Champions	2008
NL West Champions	2009

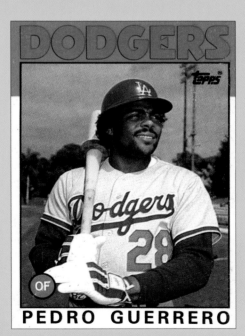

PEDRO GUERRERO

TOP: Dusty Baker led the 1981 club with a .320 average. **RIGHT**: Pedro Guerrero led the 1983 and 1985 Dodgers in home runs.

PINPOINTS

The history of a baseball team is made up of many smaller stories. These stories take place all over the map—not just in the city a team calls "home." Match the pushpins on these maps to the **TEAM FACTS**, and you will begin to see the story of the Dodgers unfold!

1 Los Angeles, California—*The team has played here since 1958.*

2 Tacoma, Washington—*Ron Cey was born here.*

3 Chicago, Illinois—*The Dodgers won the 1959 World Series here.*

4 Princeton, Indiana—*Gil Hodges was born here.*

5 Minneapolis, Minnesota—*The Dodgers won the 1965 World Series here.*

6 Hamilton, Missouri—*Zack Wheat was born here.*

7 Brooklyn, New York—*The team played here from 1884 to 1957.*

8 Washington, D.C.—*Maury Wills was born here.*

9 Cairo, Georgia—*Jackie Robinson was born here.*

10 Navojoa, Mexico—*Fernando Valenzuela was born here.*

11 Santo Domingo, Dominican Republic—*Ramon Martinez was born here.*

12 Osaka, Japan—*Hideo Nomo was born here.*

Hideo Nomo

GLOSSARY

🧠 **AMERICAN ASSOCIATION (AA)**—A rival to the National League in the 1800s. The AA played from 1882 to 1891.

🧠 *BATTLE OF LONG ISLAND*—The first major battle of the American Revolution. It was fought in August of 1776.

🧠 **BIG-LEAGUE**—The top level of professional baseball.

🧠 **COMPLETE GAMES**—Games started and finished by the same pitcher.

🧠 **CY YOUNG AWARD**—The award given each year to each league's best pitcher.

🧠 *DECADE*—A period of 10 years; also specific periods, such as the 1950s.

🧠 **DRAFTED**—Selected during the annual meeting at which teams take turns choosing the best players in high school and college.

🧠 *ECSTATIC*—Feeling great joy.

🧠 *GENERATION*—A periods of years roughly equal to the time it takes for a person to be born, grow up, and have children.

🧠 **HALL OF FAME**—The museum in Cooperstown, New York, where baseball's greatest players are honored.

🧠 *INTEGRATE*—Bring people of different races and backgrounds into one group.

🧠 **LEADOFF HITTER**—The first hitter in a lineup, or the first hitter in an inning.

🧠 **MINOR-LEAGUE**—The many professional leagues that help develop players for the big leagues.

🧠 **MOST VALUABLE PLAYER (MVP)**—The award given each year to each league's top player; an MVP is also selected for the World Series and the All-Star Game.

🧠 **NATIONAL LEAGUE (NL)**—The older of the two major leagues; the NL began play in 1876 and the American League (AL) started in 1901.

🧠 **NATIONAL LEAGUE CHAMPIONSHIP SERIES (NLCS)**—The playoff series that has decided the National League pennant since 1969.

🧠 **NO-HITTER**—A game in which a team does not get a hit.

🧠 *PEDESTRIANS*—People who travel by foot.

🧠 **PENNANT**—A league championship. The term comes from the triangular flag awarded to each season's champion, beginning in the 1870s.

🧠 **PERFECT GAME**—A game in which no batter reaches base.

🧠 **PLAYOFFS**—The games played after the regular season to determine which teams will advance to the World Series.

🧠 **POSTSEASON**—The games played after the regular season, including the playoffs and World Series.

🧠 **ROOKIE OF THE YEAR**—The annual award given to each league's best first-year player.

🧠 **RUNS BATTED IN (RBIs)**—A statistic that counts the number of runners a batter drives home.

🧠 **SAVED**—Recorded the last out or outs in a team's win. A relief pitcher on the mound at the end of a close victory is credited with a "save."

🧠 **SHUTOUTS**—Games in which one team does not score a run.

🧠 *TRADITION*—A belief or custom that is handed down from generation to generation.

🧠 **WORLD SERIES**—The world championship series played between the American League and National League pennant winners.

🧠 *WORLD WAR II*—The war between the major powers of Europe, Asia, and North America that lasted from 1939 to 1945. The United States entered the war in 1941.

EXTRA INNINGS

TEAM SPIRIT introduces a great way to stay up to date with your team! Visit our **EXTRA INNINGS** link and get connected to the latest and greatest updates. **EXTRA INNINGS** serves as a young reader's ticket to an exclusive web page—with more stories, fun facts, team records, and photos of the Dodgers. Content is updated during and after each season. The **EXTRA INNINGS** feature also enables readers to send comments and letters to the author! Log onto:

www.norwoodhousepress.com/library.aspx

and click on the tab: **TEAM SPIRIT** to access **EXTRA INNINGS**.

Read all the books in the series to learn more about professional sports. For a complete listing of the baseball, basketball, football, and hockey teams in the **TEAM SPIRIT** series, visit our website at:

www.norwoodhousepress.com/library.aspx

ON THE ROAD

LOS ANGELES DODGERS
1000 Elysian Park Avenue
Los Angeles, California 90012
(323) 224-1500
losangeles.dodgers.mlb.com

NATIONAL BASEBALL
HALL OF FAME AND MUSEUM
25 Main Street
Cooperstown, New York 13326
(888) 425-5633
www.baseballhalloffame.org

ON THE BOOKSHELF

To learn more about the sport of baseball, look for these books at your library or bookstore:

• Augustyn, Adam (editor). *The Britannica Guide to Baseball*. New York, NY: Rosen Publishing, 2011.

• Dreier, David. *Baseball: How It Works*. North Mankato, MN: Capstone Press, 2010.

• Stewart, Mark. *Ultimate 10: Baseball*. New York, NY: Gareth Stevens Publishing, 2009.

ABOUT THE AUTHOR

MARK STEWART has written more than 50 books on baseball and over 150 sports books for kids. He grew up in New York City during the 1960s rooting for the Yankees and Mets, and was lucky enough to meet players from both teams. Mark comes from a family of writers. His grandfather was Sunday Editor of *The New York Times,* and his mother was Articles Editor of *Ladies' Home Journal* and *McCall's.* Mark has profiled hundreds of athletes over the past 25 years. He has also written several books about his native New York and New Jersey, his home today. Mark is a graduate of Duke University, with a degree in history. He lives and works in a home overlooking Sandy Hook, New Jersey. You can contact Mark through the Norwood House Press website.

ML   3/12